Master Maths

MEASURE UP

Length, mass, capacity, time and money

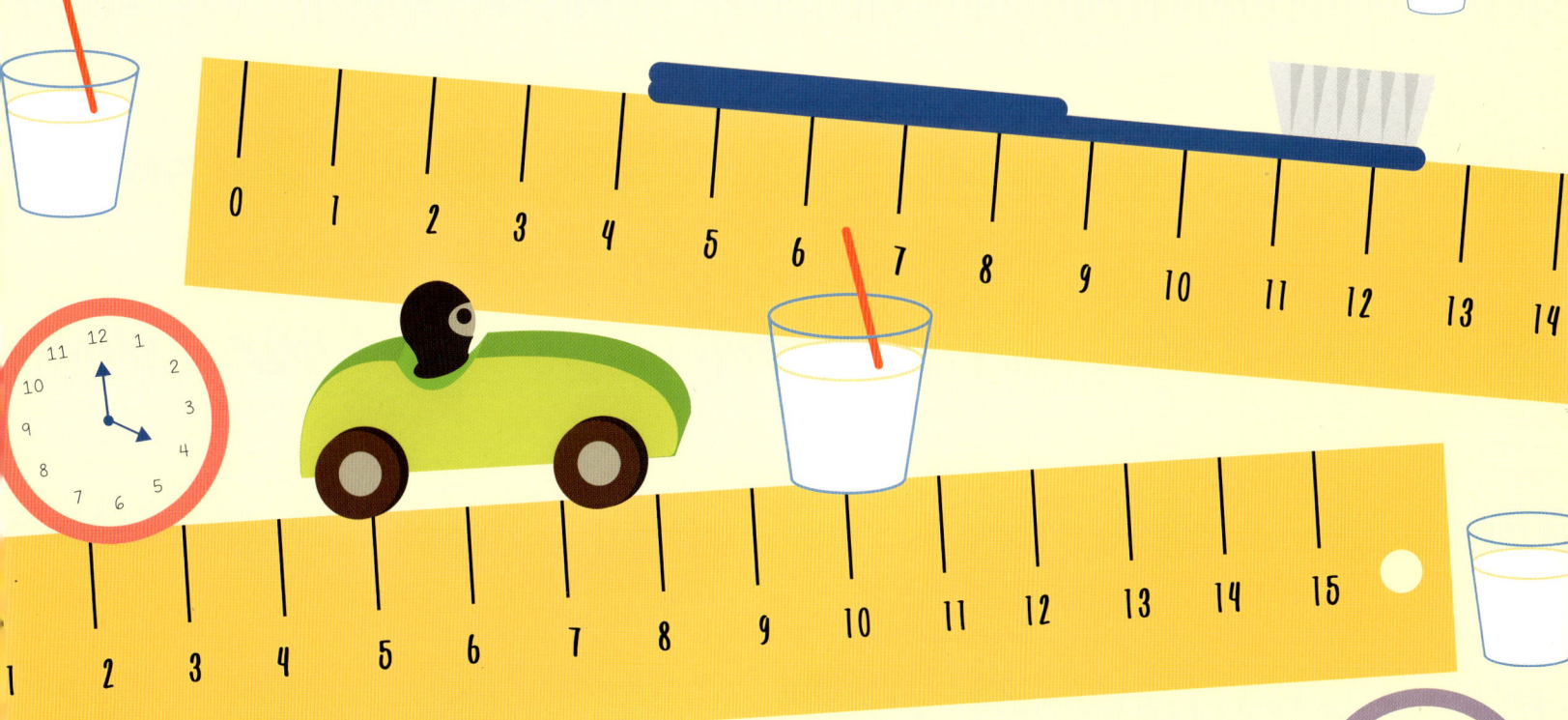

ANJANA CHATTERJEE   ILLUSTRATED BY JO SAMWAYS

CONSULTATION BY
RUTH BULL, BSc (HONS), PGCE, MA (ED)

QED

Author: Anjana Chatterjee
Consultant: Ruth Bull, BSc (HONS), PGCE, MA (ED)
Designers: emojo design and Victoria Kimonidou
Illustrator: Jo Samways
Editors: Claire Watts and Ellie Brough

© 2018 Quarto Publishing plc
First Published in 2018 by QED Publishing,
an imprint of The Quarto Group.
The Old Brewery, 6 Blundell Street,
London N7 9BH, United Kingdom.
T (0)20 7700 6700 F (0)20 7700 8066
www.QuartoKnows.com

All rights reserved. No part of this publication may be reproduced, stored in a retrieval system, or transmitted in any form or by any means, electronic, mechanical, photocopying, recording, or otherwise, without the prior permission of the publisher, nor be otherwise circulated in any form of binding or cover other than that in which it is published and without a similar condition being imposed on the subsequent purchaser.

A catalogue record for this book is available from the British Library.

ISBN 978 1 78493 934 2

9 8 7 6 5 4 3 2 1

Manufactured in DongGuan, China TL102017

> Hello, my name is Pango. I'm a pangolin and I love maths! I'll be your guide to becoming a maths master!

CONTENTS

Unit 1 Long, short, tall ....page 4
Unit 2 Heavy and light ....page 10
Unit 3 How much is inside? ....page 14
Unit 4 Time ....page 18
Unit 5 Looking at money ....page 26
Tools for success ....page 32

HOW TO USE THE BOOKS IN THIS SERIES

The four books in Year 1 of the Master Maths series focus on the main strands of the curriculum but using the leading Singapore maths approach. This method involves teaching children to think and explain mathematically, with an emphasis on problem solving, focusing on the following three-step approach:

1 Concrete
Children engage in hands-on learning activities using concrete objects such as counters, cubes, dice, paper clips or buttons. For example, children might add 4 cubes and 3 cubes together.

2 Pictorial
Children draw pictorial representations of mathematical concepts. For example, children might draw a number bond diagram showing that 3 and 4 together make 7.

3 Abstract
Children can then move on to solving mathematical problems in an abstract way by using numbers and symbols. Once children understand that 3 and 4 make 7 when they are added together, they can use the abstract method to record it.

$3 + 4 = 7$

Each unit of the book begins with a question or statement that encourages children to begin thinking about a new mathematical concept. This is followed by visual explanations and hands-on activities that lead children to a deep conceptual understanding. Children should repeat and vary the activities, and be encouraged to revisit earlier sections to seek clarification and to deepen their understanding. You will find extension activities and further instruction in the Parent and Teacher Guidance sections.

UNIT 1 LONG, SHORT, TALL

When we talk about how long and short things are, we are talking about **length**.

Look at the pictures.

The green pencil is **long**.
The red pencil is **short**.

The yellow scarf is long.
The orange scarf is short.

Can you find a long pencil and a short pencil?

COMPARE THE LENGTHS

Compare the length of some things from your pencil case.
Line up a pencil and a rubber so they have the same starting point.

ends lined up →

Which object is long?
Which object is short?

The pencil is **longer** than the rubber.
The rubber is **shorter** than the pencil.

PARENT AND TEACHER GUIDANCE
- Remind children that in order to compare lengths they need to line up one end of the objects they are comparing.

Now line up 3 things.

The pencil is **longest**.
The rubber is **shortest**.

4 **VOCABULARY:** length, long, short, compare, longer, shorter, longest, shortest

SHORT AND TALL

When we talk about how short or **tall** something is, we are talking about **height**.

The cereal box is tall.
The juice carton is short.

Let's compare these 3 bears.
The blue bear is **taller** than the green bear.
The brown bear is shorter than the green bear.
Which bear is **tallest**?
Which bear is shortest?

HOW LONG?

Let's **measure** with paper clips.

The paintbrush is the same length as 8 paper clips.
We can say that the paintbrush is 8 paper clips long.

TRY THIS:
Measure some more objects.
How many teaspoons long is your book?
How many crayons high is the table?

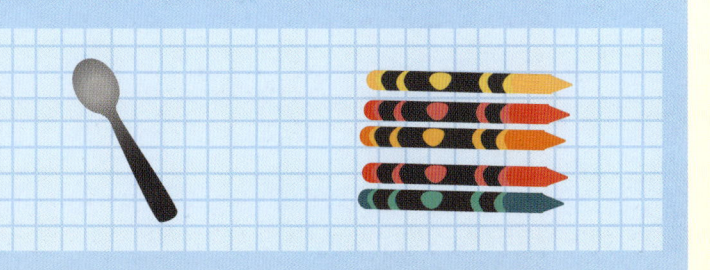

PARENT AND TEACHER GUIDANCE
- Before children move on to measure using standard measures, they need lots of practice in using non-standard units, such as paper clips, toy cars or crayons.

VOCABULARY: tall, height, taller, tallest, measure

5

MEASURING AND COMPARING

We can measure length and height in lots of different ways.
We call the thing we're using to measure the **unit** of measurement.

handspans

feet

paces

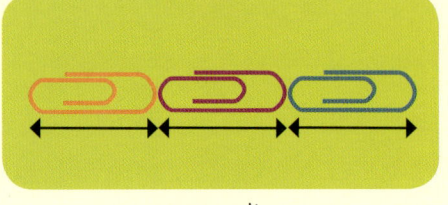

paperclips

bricks

pencils

DIFFERENT OBJECTS, SAME UNIT

Look at the paintbrushes
Which paintbrush is longer?
How do you know?

Measure some different objects with the same unit.
Say which is longer and which is shorter.

SAME OBJECT, DIFFERENT UNITS

Look at the cereal box.
How many juice cartons high is the cereal box?
How many cans high is the cereal box?

Measure an object with two or more different units.
Why do you think the number of units is different
each time?

VOCABULARY: unit

MEASURING IN CENTIMETRES

Let's find out how to measure using a **ruler**.
Look at the marks on this ruler.
Each mark shows a **centimetre**.

> A centimetre is always the same length on any ruler.

A centimetre is a unit of measurement.
We can use this ruler to measure things in centimetres.
We use a ruler to measure things **accurately**.

TRY THIS:

Line a crayon up with the line marked 0 on the ruler.
Find the mark nearest to the other end of the crayon.
That shows you how long the crayon is in centimetres.
This crayon is 10 centimetres long.

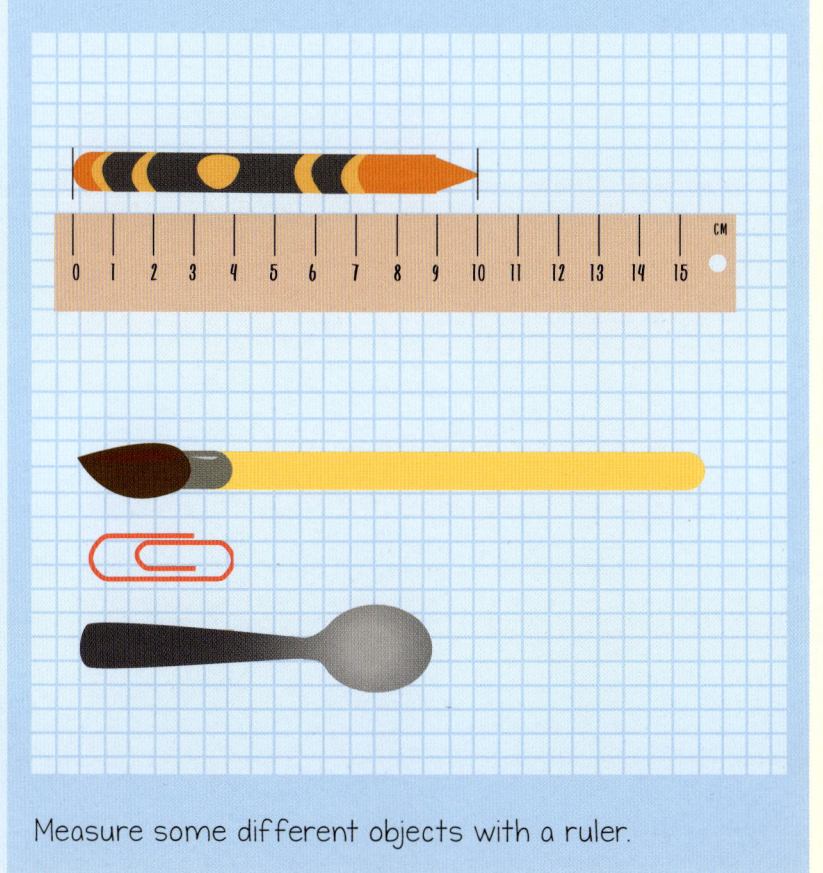

Measure some different objects with a ruler.

PARENT AND TEACHER GUIDANCE

- As children measure different objects with the same unit, they will see that different-sized objects give different measurements.

- As children measure the same object with different units, they will see that they will need different numbers of units.

- Remind children to express the unit of measurement when they measure. For example, "The pencil is 8 centimetres long" or "The pencil is 8 rubbers long" rather than "The pencil measures 8."

VOCABULARY: ruler, centimetre, accurate

MEASURING IN METRES

When we measure things that are very long or very tall we use a different unit. We use a longer unit called a **metre**.

A metre is the same as 100 centimetres.

We can use a **metre stick** to measure metres.
Each small mark on the metre stick is one centimetre.

We can also measure in metres with a **measuring tape**.
Can you see the centimetre marks?

TRY THIS:
Can you use metre sticks or a measuring tape to measure a room in metres?
Find something longer than a metre. Now find something shorter than a metre.

PARENT AND TEACHER GUIDANCE
- At this stage children will be looking at whole metres and centimetres only. Real-world measuring may raise questions about this. Use language such as "a bit more than", "a bit less than", "and a bit", "nearly", "almost" or "over".

VOCABULARY: metre, metre stick, measuring tape

TIME TO PRACTISE!

Let's do some measuring.

How many centimetres long is each object? Look at the ruler beneath each object to find the object's length.

Which is longer, the rubber or the toy car? Which of the 3 objects is the longest? Which object is the shortest?

Use a ruler to find an object that is longer than the toothbrush. Now find something that is shorter than the rubber.

TRY THIS:
How long is this table?
Use a metre stick to find an object that is longer than the table. Now find something that is shorter than the table.

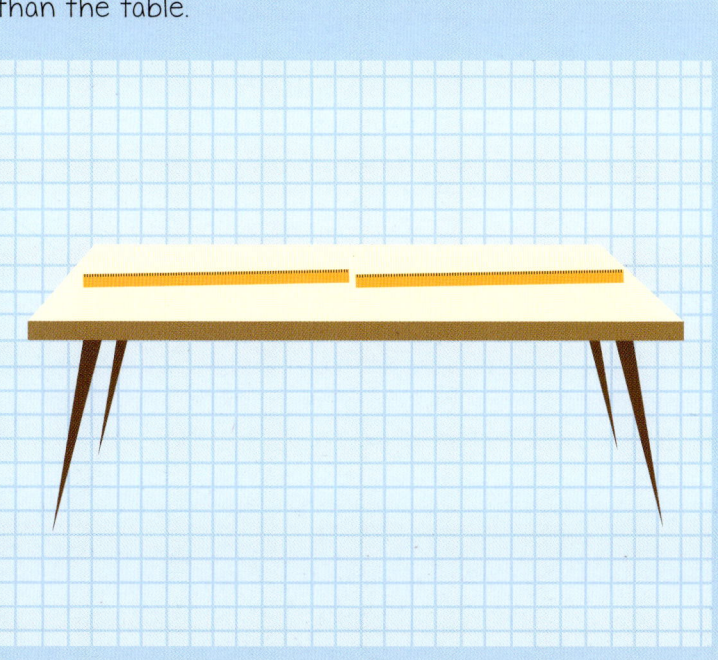

PARENT AND TEACHER GUIDANCE
- Children need plenty of practice with measuring length before tackling height.
- Children could use string cut into metre lengths for measuring if you do not have metre sticks.
- Discuss the difference between length, width and height with children.

Now try measuring how high a table is.

UNIT 2 — HEAVY AND LIGHT

When we talk about how **heavy** or **light** something is, we are talking about **weight** or **mass**.

Look at the book and the pencil.

The book is heavy.
The pencil is light.

The book is **heavier** than the pencil.
The pencil is **lighter** than the book.

Pick up this book. Do you think it's heavy?

COMPARING WEIGHT

Find two objects you can hold in your hands.

Which one is heavier?
Which one is lighter?

Choose some other objects.
Here are some things you could try.
What is the **heaviest** object you have found?
What is the **lightest** object?

PARENT AND TEACHER GUIDANCE

- At this stage, the words "mass" and "weight" may be used interchangeably.

- Prompt children to discover that they will have to compare each object with several others to discover the heaviest and the lightest.

VOCABULARY: heavy, light, weight, mass, heavier, lighter, heaviest, lightest

THINK ABOUT IT

Let's look at some different objects and compare how heavy they are.

Look at the pictures.

Which object is heavy?
Which object is light?

You can't hold all these objects in your hands, so you will have to think hard!

car

bicycle

strawberry

watermelon

baby

grown-up

PARENT AND TEACHER GUIDANCE
- Mass is a more complex measure for children than length because it cannot be visualised and because direct comparison of the mass of objects is imprecise unless a balance is used.
- Use household objects or toys to demonstrate to children that objects are not always heavier just because they are bigger.

MEASURING WEIGHT

We can use a **balance** to compare the weight of objects.

This is a balance.

What happens to the balance when we put a pencil and a juice carton in the pans?

The juice carton has gone down.
That shows that it is heavier than the pencil.

The pencil has gone up.
That shows that it is lighter than the juice carton.

BALANCED BALANCE

Look at this balance. What do you notice?

The pans on each side are at the same level.
The pans are balanced.

When the pans are balanced, the mass of the objects in each pan is the same.
So we know the marker pen has the same mass as 6 cubes.
The marker pen **weighs** the same as 6 cubes.

Try finding the mass of some other objects using cubes and a balance.
Try using different objects to measure mass with.

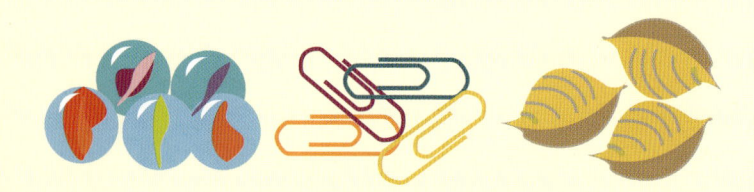

marbles   paper clips   pasta shells

PARENT AND TEACHER GUIDANCE

- Children should have an understanding of what mass or weight means before they begin to use a balance to compare the mass of objects.

12   VOCABULARY: balance, weigh

COMPARING MASS

Let's practise comparing the mass of objects.

How many cubes does the packet of crayons weigh?
Do you think it is lighter or heavier than a ruler?
How could you check?

You could compare the ruler and the crayons on the balance.

You could compare both objects with cubes.
The crayons weigh 5 cubes.
The ruler weighs 1 cube.
So the crayons weigh more than the ruler.
The crayons are heavier than the ruler.

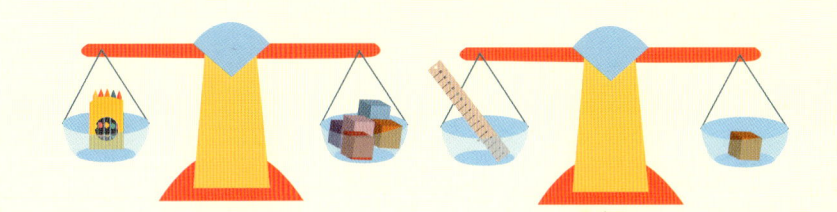

GRAMS AND KILOGRAMS

When we are measuring mass, the units we use are called **grams** and **kilograms**.

You can use weights like these on one side of the balance to measure mass.

This apple weighs 100 grams.
Use gram weights to weigh an apple.
Can you find something heavier than the apple?
Can you find something lighter?

PARENT AND TEACHER GUIDANCE

- Encourage children to estimate before they compare mass. Ask questions such as: "Which do you think is heavier: the big, empty bottle or the small, full bottle?"

- Point out to children that food packets usually show the mass of the contents in grams. Can they look at different packets and say which is heavier?

- Show children different types of weighing scales and ask them to work out how they can use the scale to measure mass.

VOCABULARY: grams, kilograms

UNIT 3 — HOW MUCH IS INSIDE?

Let's look at how much space there is inside things.

Look at this jug.
How would you describe it?

This jug is **empty**.
It has nothing inside it.

Look around you for some objects that have space inside them, such as boxes, cups and jugs.

Look at this jug.
How would you describe it?

This jug is **full**.
This jug has juice inside it.
It is full of juice.

Look at this jug.
How would you describe it?

This jug is **half full**.
This jug has some juice inside it.
It has less juice than the full jug.
It has more juice than the empty jug.

PARENT AND TEACHER GUIDANCE

- Show children two bottles, one full of water and one empty. Ask, "What's the difference between these bottles?"

- Give children empty cups and a bottle of water. Ask them to show you a full cup, an empty cup, a cup that's half full and two cups that have more and less water in them.

VOCABULARY: empty, full, half full

WHICH HOLDS MOST?

Let's look at how much water different bottles can **hold**.

1. Look at the bottles. Which bottle do you think will hold the most? Why? Which bottle do you think will hold the least? Why?

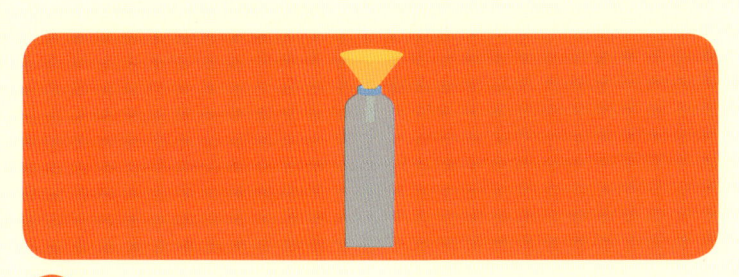

2. Take one of your empty bottles and place the funnel in the top.

3. Fill the cup with water and pour it into the bottle. Pour in more cups of water until the bottle is full. Carefully count how many cups of water you use to fill the bottle.

YOU WILL NEED:
- some bottles in different sizes
- a funnel
- a cup
- a marker pen

4. Write the number of cups on the bottle with the marker pen.

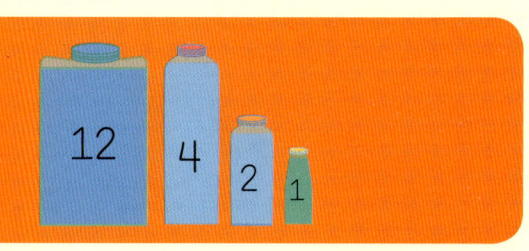

5. Do this with the other bottles. Can you put them in order from the bottle that holds the most to the bottle that holds the least?

You can play this game with lots of **containers**. Try milk containers and yogurt pots.

PARENT AND TEACHER GUIDANCE
- Capacity is an abstract concept, so children need a lot of guidance. Use different sized cups to ask questions such as, "Which cup do you think holds most?" "Which cup holds least?"

VOCABULARY: hold, container

DIFFERENT CONTAINERS

We use containers such as jugs, cups, mugs, bottles and buckets to hold liquids like water, milk and juice.

Here are some different containers.

Can you think of some more types of containers?

The bucket holds enough water to fill 9 glasses.

The jug holds enough juice to fill 4 glasses.

TRY THIS:
Look at these bottles.

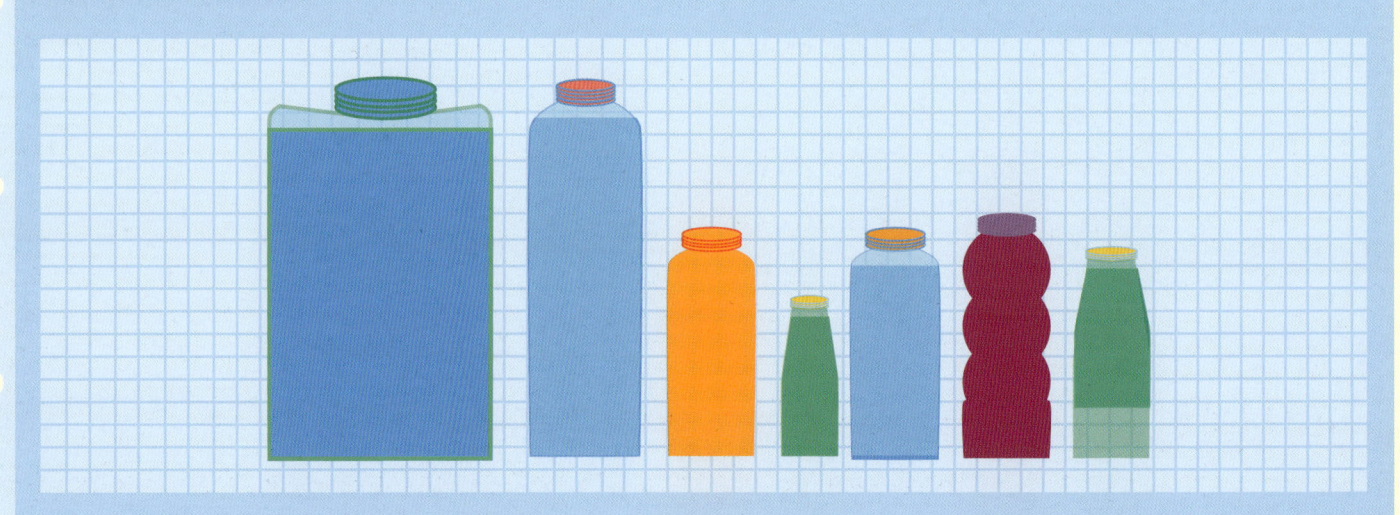

What is different about the bottles?
What is the same about the bottles?
Which bottle do you think holds the most water? Can you explain why?

THINK ABOUT IT

Let's think about how much things contain.

Look at the milk container.
One container can fill 5 glasses with milk.

How many glasses do you think 2 containers can fill?
2 containers can fill 10 glasses.

How many glasses do you think 3 containers can fill?

HOW MUCH DOES IT HOLD?

The amount a container can hold is called its **capacity**. Which bottle holds more paint?

The big bottle of paint can fill 8 paint pots. The big bottle has the same capacity as 8 paint pots.

The small bottle of paint can fill 4 paint pots. The small bottle has the same capacity as 4 paint pots.

The big bottle holds more paint than the small bottle.
The small bottle holds less paint than the big bottle.

PARENT AND TEACHER GUIDANCE
- At this stage, you may find the words "capacity" and "volume" used interchangeably. Capacity refers to the amount of space inside something. Volume is the amount of space something takes up.

VOCABULARY: capacity

UNIT 4 TIME

When we talk about when things happen or how long they take, we are talking about **time**.

> The **first** thing I do every morning is eat my breakfast.

When you get out of bed, it is usually light outside. It is the **morning**.

It's breakfast time. What will you do **next**? You might go to school.

Soon it's **night**. The sky is dark and you might see the moon or stars. It's bedtime.

Later, you will have lunch. **After** lunch, it is the **afternoon**. You might play.

Later on, it starts to get dark. It's time for tea or supper. It's the **evening**.

PARENT AND TEACHER GUIDANCE
- Talk to children regularly about things they have done, things they do regularly and things they are going to do. Prompt them to use time vocabulary.

VOCABULARY: time, first, morning, next, later, after, afternoon, evening, soon, night

WHAT HAPPENED?

Let's look at how things happen in order.

These pictures are in the wrong order.

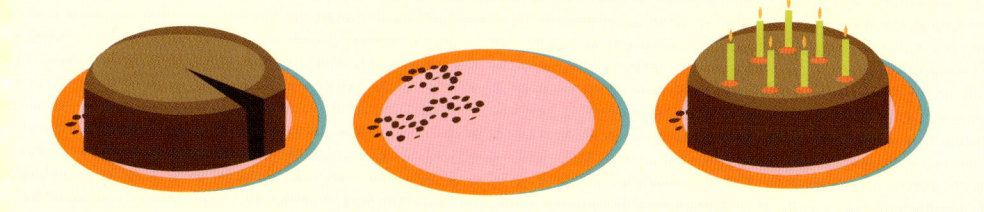

What happened first?
What happened next?
What happened **last**?

TALK ABOUT IT

Talk about your day with your friend.

Here are some time words you can use: first, next, **then**, after, **before**

What did you do after breakfast?
When did you clean your teeth?
What was the first thing you did?
Did you get up in the morning, the afternoon or the evening?
What meal do you eat in the evening?
What did you do before lunch?

VOCABULARY: last, then, before

19

DAYS, WEEKS, MONTHS AND YEARS

We measure time in **days, weeks, months** and **years**.

Every morning when you wake up a new day starts.
There are 7 days in a week.

| Monday | Tuesday | Wednesday | Thursday | Friday | Saturday | Sunday |

The days of the week always come in this order.
After Sunday, you start again with Monday.

DAYS OF THE WEEK

Let's make a circle to show the order of the days of the week.

YOU WILL NEED:
- sticky notes
- a long strip of paper
- paper clips

1. Write the days of the week on sticky notes. Stick the notes in order along a long strip of paper.

2. Using two paper clips, join the ends of the strip of paper together with the words on the outside.

3. What day is it **today**? Turn the pad of sticky notes so that the sticky strip is at the bottom. Write the word "today" and stick it at the top of today's name.

4. We call the day before today **yesterday**. What day was it yesterday? Add a sticky note to mark yesterday.

5. We call the day after today **tomorrow**. Add a sticky note to tomorrow.

VOCABULARY: day, week, month, year, today, yesterday, tomorrow

MONTHS OF THE YEAR

Let's look at the months of the year.

This is a **calendar**.

This calendar shows the month of February.
There are 12 months in a year.
Can you see the names of the days of the week on the calendar?

February usually has only 28 days.
Most of the months are 30 or 31 days long.

Which month comes after February?
Which month comes before July?
Which month comes after December?

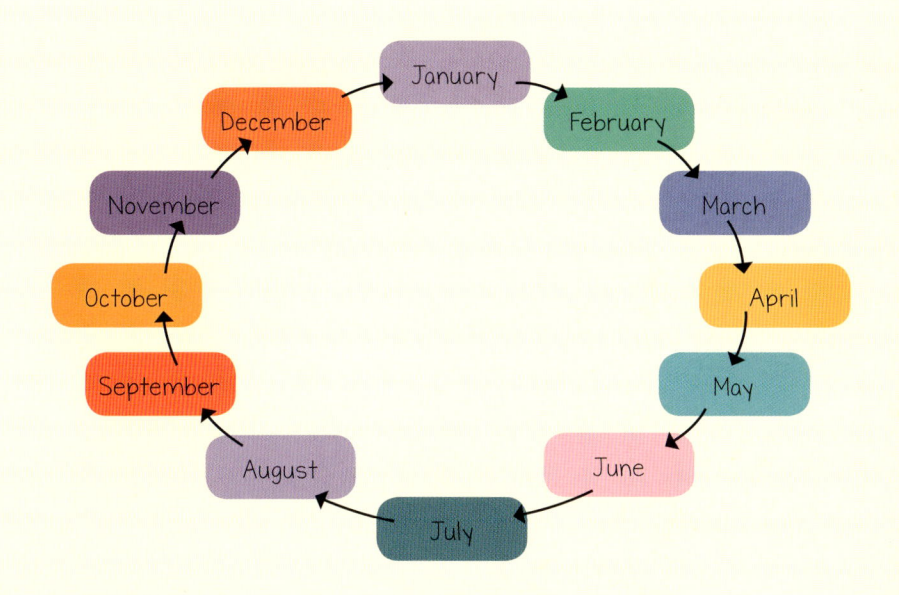

FEBRUARY

Sunday	Monday	Tuesday	Wednesday	Thursday	Friday	Saturday
1	2	3	4	5	6	7
8	9	10	11	12	13	14
15	16	17	18	19	20	21
22	23	24	25	26	27	28

January → February → March → April → May → June → July → August → September → October → November → December → January

BIRTHDAYS

Everyone has a birthday once a year.
It's a celebration of the day they were born.

This boy is 6 years old.
He is celebrating his 6th birthday.
How many years old are you?

Do you know when your birthday is?

VOCABULARY: calendar

21

CLOCK TIME

We now know how to measure time in months, weeks and days. We use a **clock** to measure smaller bits of time. There are lots of different types of clocks.

> Look around your home and see how many different clocks you can find.

MINUTES AND HOURS

Clocks measure **minutes** and **hours**.

On this clock, the small **hand** points to the hours.
The big hand points to the minutes.

On this clock, the number on the left shows the hours.
The number on the right shows the minutes.

TRY THIS:
Watch the hands on a clock as they move.
Which hand moves faster?

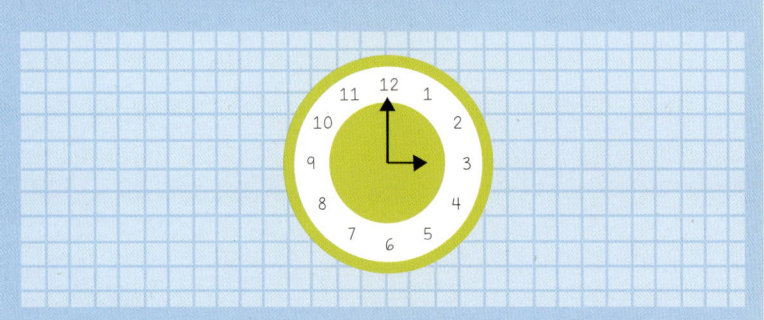

The minute hand goes faster than the hour hand. It takes one hour for the minute hand to turn right around once. In one hour, the hour hand only moves from one number to the next one.

PARENT AND TEACHER GUIDANCE
- Show children different clocks, some analogue and some digital. Discuss what is the same and what is different about them. You could ask questions such as, "How many numbers are on the clock?"

VOCABULARY: clock, minute, hour, hand

TELLING THE TIME

Let's find out how to read the time on a clock.

1 Look at the minute hand of the clock. When the minute hand points straight up, it is the beginning of a new hour. The time is something **o'clock**.

2 The hour hand points to the hours. The hour hand on this clock is pointing to the 4.

3 The time is 4 o'clock.

1 On this clock, first look at the number on the left. The left number tells us the hours.

2 The right number shows the minutes. Two zeroes mean that no minutes have passed. It is something o'clock.

3 The time is 11 o'clock.

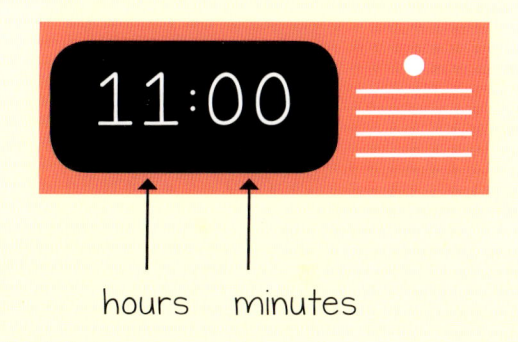

WHAT CAN YOU DO?

Some clocks have another hand that measures smaller units of time called **seconds**. The second hand moves very fast.

What can you do in a second?
What can you do in a minute?
What can you do in an hour?
Ask an adult to help you find out the answers.

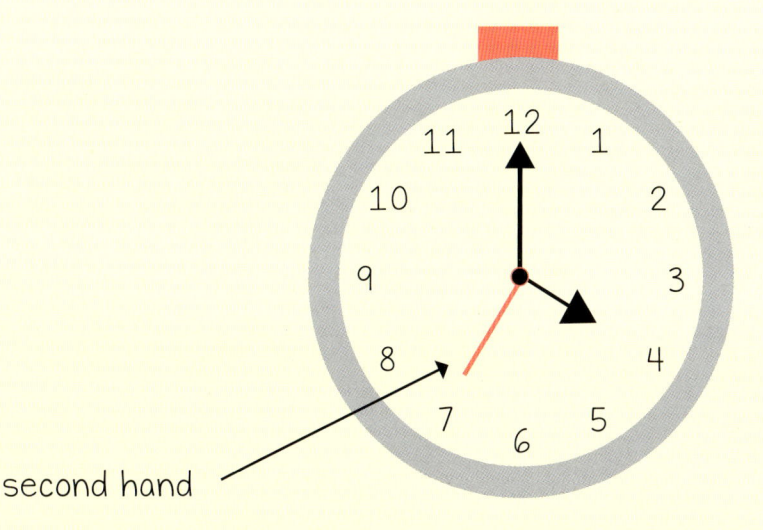

VOCABULARY: o'clock, second

WHAT TIME IS IT?

Read the time on the clocks.

Pippa is going to bed.
What time is it?

Pippa is playing in the garden.
What time is it?

It's time for breakfast.
What time is it?

8:00

It's time for a snack.
What time is it?

10:00

TRY THIS:
Use a toy clock or draw a clock face to show these times.

School starts at 9 o'clock.   I go to bed at 8 o'clock.

What time do you go to bed?

PARENT AND TEACHER GUIDANCE
- Give children plenty of opportunities to recognise times and make them by drawing or using a geared clock.

24

HALF PAST

Let's think about a different time that a clock can show.

1. Pretend that your arm is a minute hand.
   Stand with your arm straight up.
   It's something o'clock.

2. Move your arm in a big circle the way the minute hand moves. When it's straight up again, a whole hour has passed.

3. Start with your arm straight up again.
   Move your arm half way round the circle.
   Where is it pointing now?

4. When the minute hand on a clock has turned half way round, it points straight down.
   The hour hand has moved too.
   It's half way between the 3 and the 4.
   The time is **half past** 3.

5. On this clock, half past 3 looks like this.
   The number 30 shows that the time is 30 minutes after 3 o'clock.

TRY THIS:
Can you read the time on these clocks?

PARENT AND TEACHER GUIDANCE

- Have children practise recognising and making half past times using real, drawn and toy clocks.

- Children may find the movement of the hour hand puzzling. Demonstrate that when the minute hand is at half past, the hour hand has moved exactly half way between the two hours.

VOCABULARY: half past

25

UNIT 5 LOOKING AT MONEY

We use **money** to **buy** things.
Money is made up of different **coins** and **notes**.
Each coin and note has a **value**.

Can you find any coins that are not circles?

Here are the coins we use to buy things.
The front and the back of the coins look different.

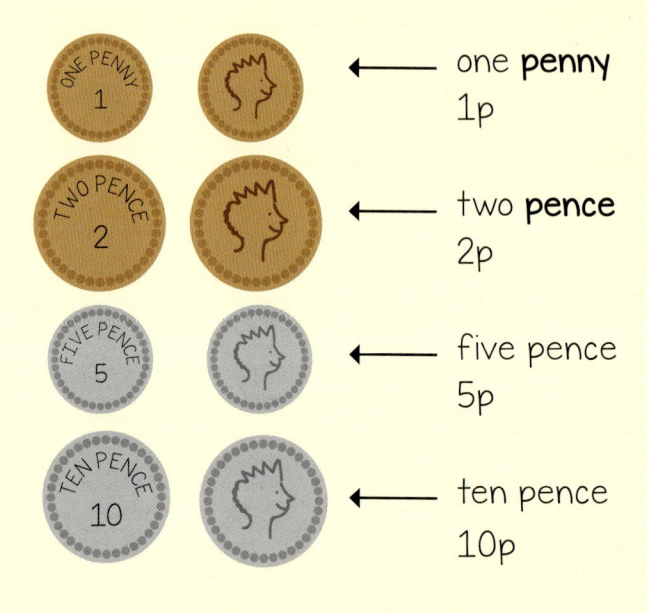

← one **penny**
1p

← two **pence**
2p

← five pence
5p

← ten pence
10p

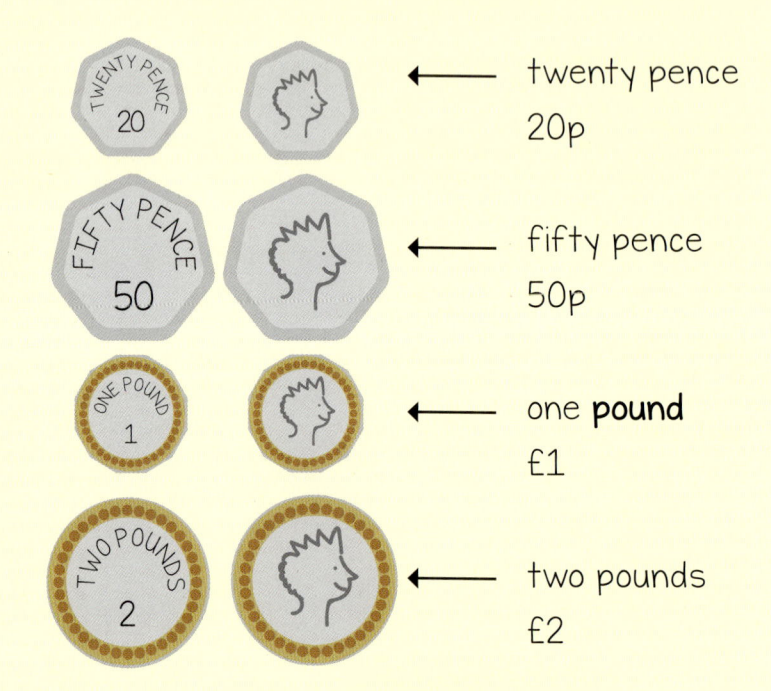

← twenty pence
20p

← fifty pence
50p

← one **pound**
£1

← two pounds
£2

Do you have a money box where you collect coins?
Open it and see how the coins look and feel.
What shape are the coins?
What colour are they?
Can you see any numbers on the coins?
Can you see any words?

PARENT AND TEACHER GUIDANCE

- Some British coins have no numbers on them and the words are written in capitals which can be difficult for young children to read. Point out the number names to children, but be aware that at this stage, they will distinguish the coins by shape and colour rather than the number.

- Give children opportunities to handle coins and notes.

VOCABULARY: money, buy, coin, note, value, penny, pence, pound

HOW MUCH ARE COINS WORTH?

Each coin has a different value.
The value tells you how much the coin is **worth**.

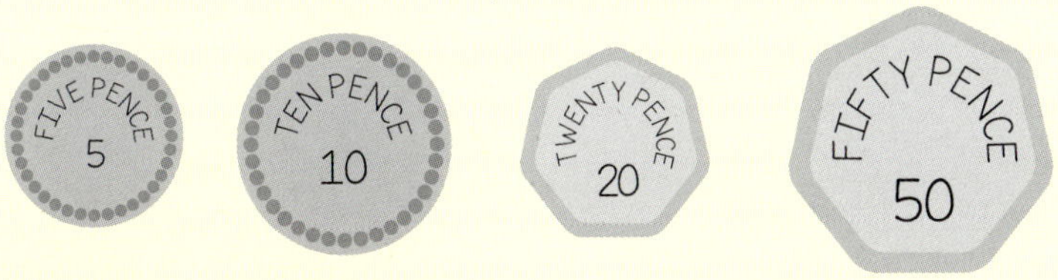

The number on a coin tells you its value.

This coin is worth one penny.

This coin is worth two pence.

So one 2p coin is worth the same as two 1p coins

2 = 1 + 1

Can you work out how many 1p coins are the same as all these coins? Draw around some coins to show your answers.

5   10   20   50

PARENT AND TEACHER GUIDANCE
- Children may notice that sometimes you pay using a card rather than with coins and notes. Explain that you keep most of your money in the bank. When you use a card, it sends a message to your bank, asking them to pay an amount of money to the seller's bank account.

POUNDS

One pound is worth 100p.

A £2 coin is worth the same as two £1 coins.

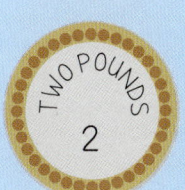

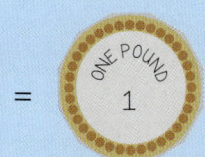

2 = 1 + 1

For greater values we use money called notes. Can you see how many pounds each of these notes is worth?

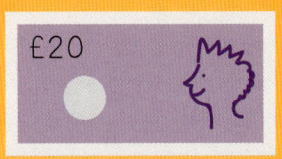

£5   £20
£10   £50

VOCABULARY: worth

27

COUNTING MONEY

Remember that coins have different values. Look carefully at the number written in words or digits on each coin.

Ask an adult to help you read the number words on the coins.

This apple costs 7p.

I can buy it with these coins.   5p + 2p = 7p

This orange costs 11p.
Which coins can I use to buy it?
Can you write an addition sentence to show this?

This watermelon costs 35p.
Which coins can I use to buy it?
Can you write an addition sentence to show this?

TRY THIS:
Add up the coins below and say which of these things you could buy with them.

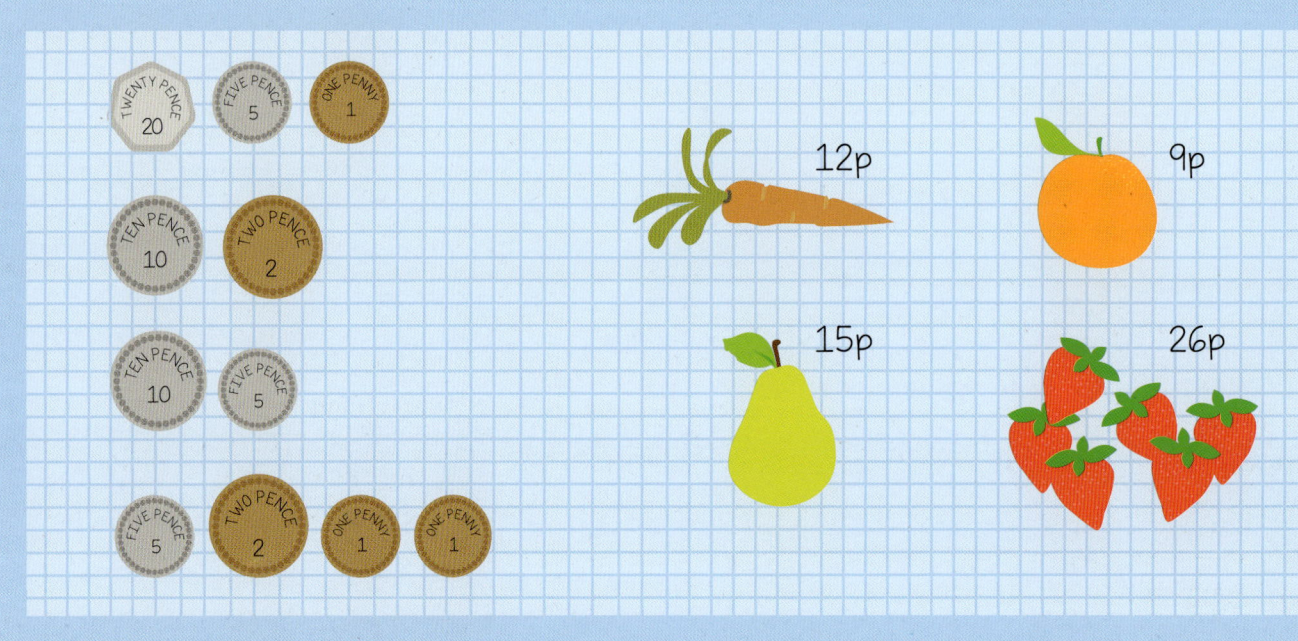

12p

9p

15p

26p

Write addition sentences to show how you added the amounts.

28

MAKE THE RIGHT AMOUNT

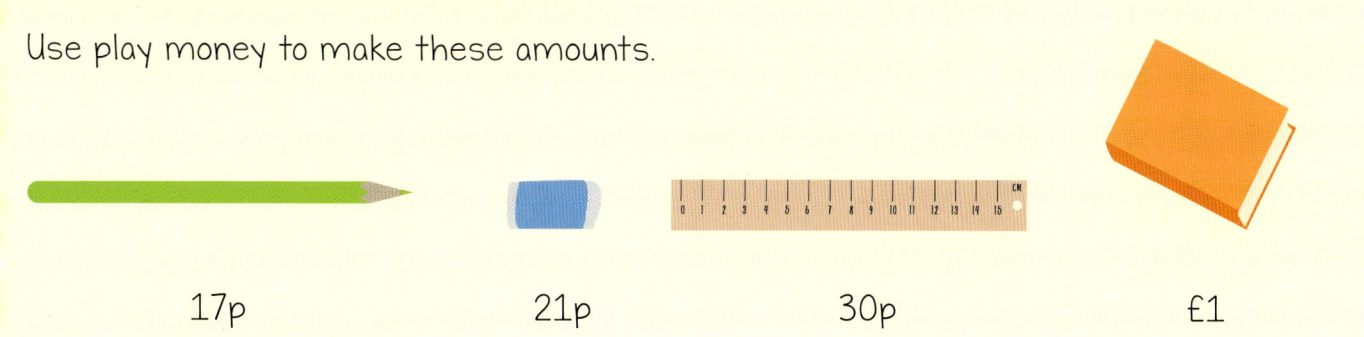

Use play money to make these amounts.

17p   21p   30p   £1

MORE OR LESS

Look at the prices of the items.

Which object costs more?
Write an addition sentence to show how you could make each amount with coins.

17p   21p

Which object costs less?
Write an addition sentence to show how you could make each amount with coins.

21p   30p

How much do 3 notebooks cost?
Can you show this amount with coins?

£1   £1   £1

Which object costs most?
Which object costs least?

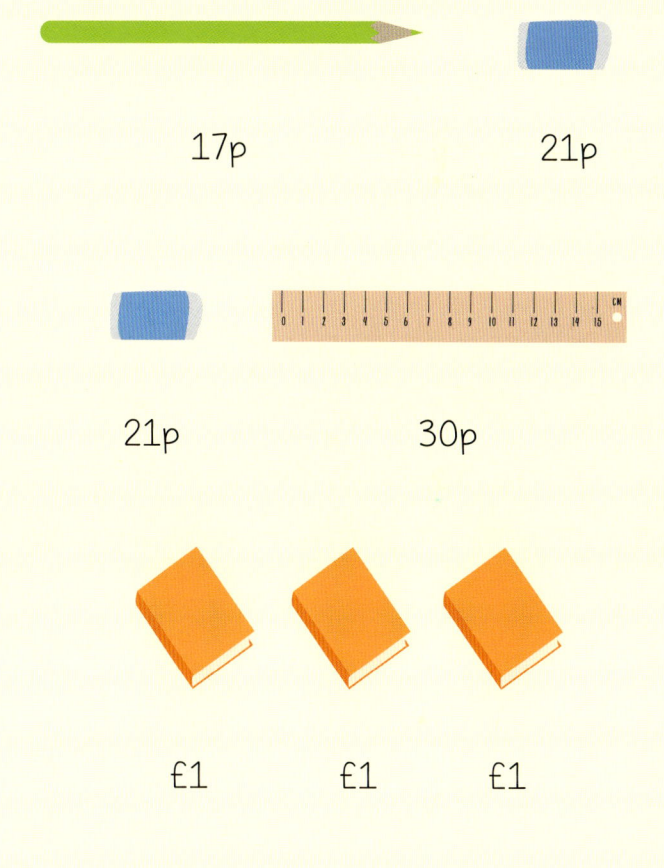

PARENT AND TEACHER GUIDANCE
- Children can use play money for these activities, or they can make play coins by drawing around real money onto stiff paper and cutting out the shapes.

ADDING WITH MONEY

Let's look at different ways to make amounts with coins.

These coins make 12p.

10p + 2p = 12p

These coins also make 12p.

5p + 5p + 1p + 1p = 12p

Can you find any more ways to make 12p?

We can make 24p with coins like this.

20p + 2p + 2p = 24p

Here's another way to make 24p.

5p + 5p + 5p + 5p + 1p + 1p + 1p + 1p = 24p

And here's another way!

10p + 10p + 2p + 2p = 24p

Can you find some more ways to make 24p?

If you can't read the words on the coins, ask a grown-up to help you.

TRY THIS:
Try making each of these amounts with coins in two different ways.

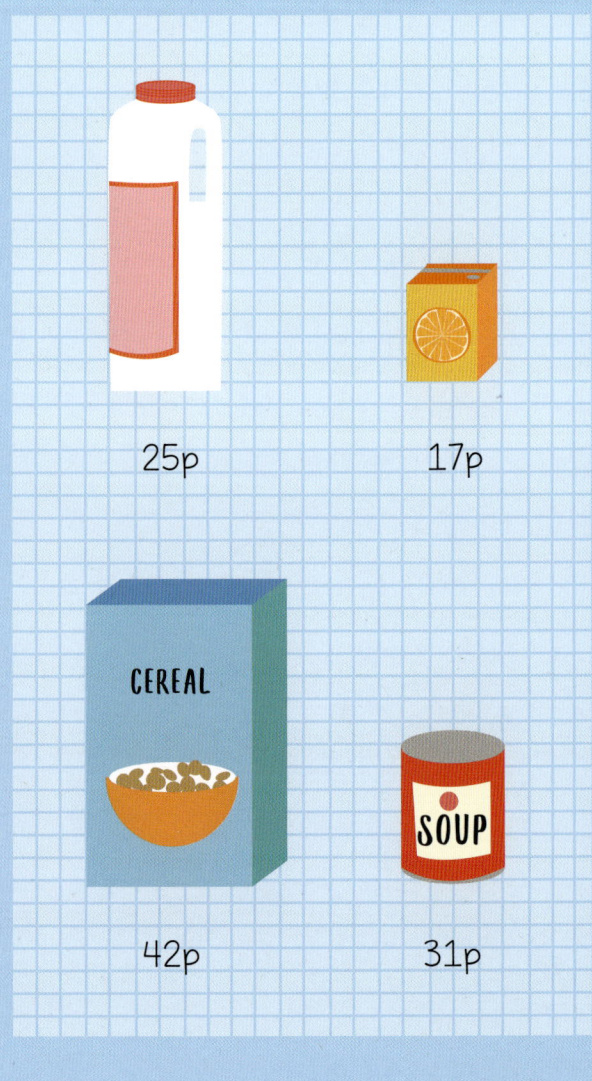

25p

17p

42p

31p

Write an addition sentence for each one to show your answers.

WHICH IS MORE?

Look at these groups of coins.

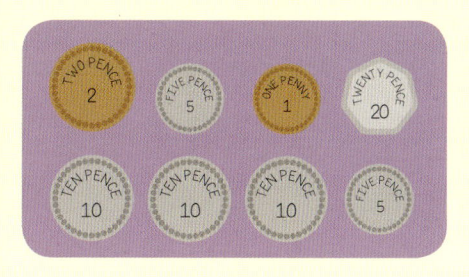

Which group is worth more? Add up the values of the coins to find out.

IS IT ENOUGH?

When we buy something, we have to give enough money.

Sometimes we give the **exact** amount.
The cookie costs 16p.
The coins are worth 16p.

If we don't have the right coins to make the exact amount, we can give more money.
The doughnut costs 18p.
The coin is worth 20p.
20p is more than 18p.

The shop will give us some other coins back as **change**.

Say if these amounts of money are enough to buy each thing.
Remember, you can pay the exact amount or you can pay more.

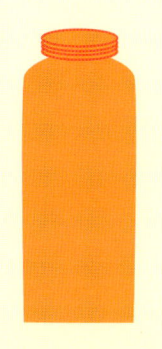

36p

14p

VOCABULARY: exact, change

31

TOOLS FOR SUCCESS

Most of the maths activities in the book can be carried out using everyday items, but the following mathematical tools are used in this book and you may find them useful.

Ruler
30-cm or 15-cm rulers, marked with centimetres only, can be used to introduce children to the concept of measuring using a scale. You should remind children how to position the ruler so that the object being measured lines up with the 0 on the ruler.

Measuring tape
A measuring tape is useful for measuring longer lengths.

Metre rule
Metre rules can be used for activities such as measuring the length of a room or a playing field. Demonstrate how to move one rule to measure a longer length or use several rules to measure. You are not looking for accurate measuring at this stage, just the concept of using units to measure.

Balance
A balance will help children to establish the idea of mass as a comparison. Use questions such as, "Which is lighter/heavier?" "How many cubes weigh the same as...?" Show children the weight measurements on packets of food and move on to using gram or kilogram weights with a balance when they seem ready.

Geared clock
A geared clock is a useful tool as the hands turn round in relation to one another in the same way as on a real clock.

Play money
A set of plastic coins and notes is a useful resource for providing children with practice of handling money.

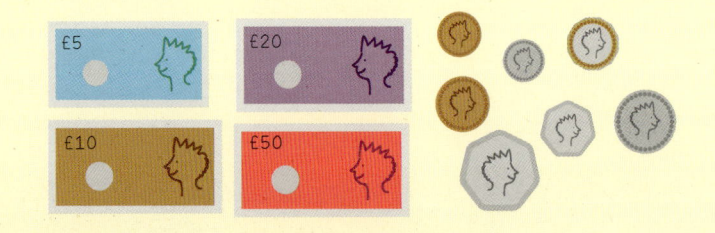